DEADLY
2013 ANNUAL

BBC
EARTH

DEADLY 💀

2013
ANNUAL

Orion
Children's Books

First published in Great Britain in 2012
by Orion Children's Books
a division of the Orion Publishing Group Ltd
Orion House
5 Upper St Martin's Lane
London WC2H 9EA
An Hachette UK Company

1 3 5 7 9 10 8 6 4 2

Photo credits (b: bottom; t: top; l: left; r: right; c: centre)
11b Nikki Waldron 2009 (from Deadly 60 Series 1); 12 © BBC 2009; 13 © BBC 2009; 14 © BBC 2009;
15t © BBC 2009; 15b James Brickell 2010 (from Deadly 60 Series 2); 16b © BBC 2009; 17t © BBC 2009;
18b © BBC 2010; 19 © BBC 2009; 20b © Getty Images; 22 © BBC 2009; 23 © BBC 2009; 24© BBC 2009;
24cl Nikki Waldron 2009 (from Deadly 60 Series 1); 26 © BBC 2009; 27 © BBC 2010; 30 © BBC 2009;
31t © BBC 2009; 31b James Brickell 2009 (from Deadly 60 Series 1); 32t © BBC 2009; 32b © BBC 2010;
33t Charlie Bingham 2010 (from Deadly 60 Series 2); 33b © BBC 2009; 34b © BBC 2009; 35 © BBC 2010;
36 Nikki Waldron 2010 (from Deadly 60 Series 2); 37 © BBC 2009; 39 Giles Badger 2010 (from Deadly 60 Series 2);
40t Charlie Bingham 2010 (from Deadly 60 Series 2); 41bl © BBC 2009; 42b © BBC 2009; 43 bl © BBC 2009;
44 © BBC 2009; 48-49 © BBC 2011 50c © BBC 2009; 51 © BBC 2009; © BBC 2011; 54 James Brickell 2009
(from Deadly 60 Series 1); 56 © BBC 2009; 59 © BBC 2009; 60-61 © BBC 2011; 62 Charlie Bingham 2010
(from Deadly 60 Series 2); 64-65 © BBC 2011; 66-67 Doodle; 69 Johnny Rogers 2010 (from Deadly 60 Series 2)

Ardea
16t Kurt Amsler; 17b Don Hadden; 18t Steve Downer; 34t Auscape; 41br M. Watson; 57 Suzi Eszterhas ; 58 Ken Lucas

Compiled by Jinny Johnson
Designed by Sue Michniewicz

A catalogue record for this book is available from the British Library.

ISBN 978 1 4440 0644 5

Printed and bound in Germany by Mohn Media

www.orionbooks.co.uk

CONTENTS

DEADLY

WELCOME

TO THE FIRST DEADLY ANNUAL!

As you all know, the Deadly 60 team have been lucky enough to
spend the last few years travelling the world in search of the deadliest
and most fascinating creatures. As ever, you're coming with us,
every step of the way.

In this annual we'll tell you about our experiences, take you
behind the scenes on some of our trips and share lots of facts about
Deadly 60 animals. And there are puzzles, games and
other fun stuff so dive in!

MEET THE TEAM

We have a fantastic team on Deadly 60.
When you're working in the crazy situations we end up in, and with
such extraordinary creatures, it's vital to really know and trust the people you're with.
And if you think it's all fun and games out there – think again!

The teamwork starts way before we get to the jungles, deserts and forests of the world.
Before we can do anything, the researchers and production crew at BBC Bristol
must research and plan every detail of the programmes, from plane tickets, accommodation
and the animals we hope to film, to the right gear to take along. You should see the kit
we need! As well as all the cameras, sound equipment and so on, there are all sorts of extras
– like the chainmail suits we had to wear when diving with Humboldt squid!
These hard-working people behind the scenes are vital to the making of Deadly 60.

Once we're on location, the crew might vary slightly according to where we are
and what we're doing, but here are some of the regulars.

CHARLIE

EMMA, CHARLIE AND LIZZIE
They're on the research team.
They also film with the second camera,
so you not only get to see me but also
the camera crew, and how they're
doing their job.

JAMES, ROSIE, NIKKI AND GILES
The producer/directors. They have the
difficult task of organising everyone.
They take all our crazy ideas about
which animals we want to film and
where and, with the help of the
researchers, make it a reality.

JOHNNY AND GRAHAM

The cameramen. Johnny and Graham are 2 of the best in the world. They have to be able to hang off ropes, trek through swamps and jungles and cope with Arctic weather, all while lugging really heavy cameras around.

TEAM IN ACTION

JOHN

The series producer. He makes sure our crazy ideas aren't too crazy, reviews all the material we've filmed and along with the producer/directors puts together a TV series that the audience really loves!

NICK AND JOHNNY WITH STEVE

NICK AND SIMON

The soundmen. The 'soundies' are our ears. They have to take all the sound – what I'm saying, the noises from the animals and from the environment – and mix it to get the right balance. They're a bit like DJs really.

WENDY Wendy is the boss. She's the one who looks at the programmes once they've been edited and decides if they're good enough. She's very important but really nice as well!

SIMON The underwater cameraman. Though both the regular cameramen can do a bit of filming underwater, there's no substitute for a full-time pro. Simon has filmed just about everything underwater, from whales, whale sharks and great whites to the tiny mantis shrimp. He's a genius.

And there are more. There's usually a local 'fixer' who knows the area and can help the team find what's needed.

THEN THERE'S THE EQUIPMENT

We have to take loads of technical stuff along, but here are a few
of the other items the Deadly team wouldn't be without.

BINOCULARS

Essential for every naturalist.
I'm never without mine.

SNAKE STICK/TONGS

One of the essentials. Handling venomous
snakes can be very dangerous indeed.
The hook is generally used to lift up non-
venomous snakes, or to restrain venomous
ones so you can get hold of their head.
The tongs are the safest, but they're heavy
and clunky for long jungle treks.

CAMOUFLAGE GEAR

If you wear bright colours, heavy scents
and make a lot of noise, you won't see any
wildlife at all! It's all about being discreet
and not being seen.

DIVE GEAR

This is extremely cumbersome on land but comes into its own once you hit the water. I wear a full-face mask that allows me to talk underwater, so I can tell you about the animals I see.

HEAD-TORCH

You need light at night, and you also need your hands free to operate cameras and catch bugs and snakes, so a head-torch is essential.

GUIDEBOOKS

Never stop studying! I have thousands of animal books at home and I spend hours and hours every day learning about wildlife. As there are about 800,000 types of beetle alone, you could spend your whole life studying and never know all the facts.

Once we get home there is still a lot more work to do. Back in the edit suite, the production team have to sort through hours and hours of shot footage and put together the best bits for you to watch on television. In order to get a great 30 minute show we may have had to shoot 18 hours of footage! It's quite a job, but we love it.

15

DEADLY TOP 10 FIERCEST ANIMALS

Here is the Deadly team's list of the top 10 fiercest animals –
the ones we believe to be the most ferocious predators of all.
From the huge great white shark to the giant hornet,
these creatures are all deadly in their own worlds.

1 GREAT WHITE SHARK

The magnificent great white shark is the
master of the sea and probably the most
feared of any animal.

- Can measure more than 6 metres long
  and weigh more than 2,000 kilograms.
- Has jaws lined with 300 teeth that have
  serrated edges like bread knives.
- Super-senses allow it to smell prey such
  as seals from 5 kilometres away.

2 SALTWATER CROCODILE

This crocodile is the world's largest reptile
– and the fiercest. It can't chew, but it rips
chunks of flesh from its prey.

- Up to 7 metres long and weighs 1,000
  kilograms.
- Lies in wait for prey with only its eyes,
  ears and nostrils above the water.
- Huge strength allows it to lunge out of
  the water to seize prey and drown it.

3 LION

King of the cats, the lion is the most fearsome carnivore in Africa. It has to be strong in order to tackle prey with sharp horns and hard hooves, such as wildebeest and zebra.

- Up to 2.5 metres long.
- Strength in numbers – lions work together to bring down large, fast-running prey.
- Females do most of the hunting and males defend their pride from other males.

4 LEOPARD SEAL

A ferocious seal, this hunter lurks under the ice to ambush prey such as penguins and even other seals. It is strong and speedy and one of the top predators in Antarctica.

- Up to 3.8 metres long and weighs as much as 500 kilograms.
- Powerful jaws and long canine teeth for seizing prey. Also has specially shaped, interlocking back teeth for sieving krill (a kind of shrimp) from the water.
- A streamlined body and long flippers help it move fast in water.

5 JAPANESE GIANT HORNET

These large wasps are some of the fiercest hunters in the insect world. They kill other insects, such as honeybees, in order to feed them to their young.

- Up to 5 centimetres long with a wingspan of as much as 7.5 centimetres.
- Equipped with a stinger and produces large amounts of powerful venom.
- Can kill 40 honeybees in just a minute.

6 HUMBOLDT SQUID

This jet-propelled underwater hunter is as big as a human, super-smart and hunts in schools. It catches a wide range of fish and other sea creatures – even other Humboldts!

- Up to 2 metres long and weighs as much as 50 kilograms.
- Tentacles lined with toothed suckers for seizing prey and a fearsome parrot-like beak for tearing flesh apart.
- Able to change colour when angry or threatened.

7

HONEY BADGER

A relative of the weasel, this little animal is one of the fiercest in Africa and will face up to much larger animals. Its gets its name from its habit of raiding bees' nests to feed on the bee larvae as well as honey.

- Up to about 98 centimetres long and weighs up to 14 kilograms.
- Has a powerful stocky body and large, strong claws on its front feet for breaking into insects' nests.
- Its skin is tough to protect it from the stings and teeth of prey and it can give off a very smelly liquid if attacked.

8

TIGER SHARK

A big shark with a huge appetite, this streamlined hunter will eat just about anything – alive or dead. It preys on everything from fish, birds and seals and has been known to swallow objects such as car tyres, license plates and paint cans!

- About 4.3 metres long and weighs as much as 600 kilograms.
- Fantastic senses of smell and sight.
- Super-strong jaws with sharp serrated teeth that can even break through turtle shells.

9 POLAR BEAR

This mighty king of the far north is the largest, most powerful land predator. It manages to survive in one of the toughest environments on Earth and can hunt on land, sea-ice and in the water.

- Males can weigh 400–600 kilograms and be up to 2.6 metres long.
- Has a superb sense of smell for tracking down prey and detecting seals in their lairs under the ice. Polar bears can detect a seal a metre under the ice from a kilometre away, and have been seen walking 32 kilometres in one direction towards food they can only have smelt!

10 TIGER

A solitary hunter, the tiger relies on its stripy coat to camouflage it while it creeps up on prey. It then makes a lethal last minute dash to pounce on its prey and seize it by the neck or throat.

- The Bengal tiger is about 1.8 metres long with a 90 centimetre tail and Siberian tigers are even larger.
- Very strong front legs and long sharp claws for bringing down prey.
- Kills about 50 large animals a year and can eat 27 kilograms or more of meat in one night.

WEASEL WORDSEARCH

The animals in the weasel family might be small but they are deadly hunters. Equipped with sharp teeth and an aggressive attitude, many of them will take on creatures much larger than themselves. Can you find the names of these fierce predators in this wordsearch puzzle?

L	E	H	M	A	R	T	E	N	K	T	H
E	L	N	E	R	A	T	V	N	T	S	V
S	B	D	T	C	N	F	I	E	T	E	T
A	A	T	E	S	E	M	T	N	N	P	O
E	S	L	E	R	R	E	E	I	S	N	I
W	O	O	R	T	S	L	R	R	V	S	E
P	R	E	G	D	A	B	S	E	S	O	C
T	T	P	D	B	E	K	R	V	Q	B	Y
S	T	F	H	T	U	A	N	L	A	H	T
F	I	E	L	N	R	S	T	O	A	T	P
D	I	L	K	T	N	H	F	W	R	A	Y
H	R	E	T	T	O	A	E	S	E	Y	N

WEASEL **POLECAT** **WOLVERINE** **BADGER**
MARTEN **SEA OTTER** **SKUNK** **FERRET**
STOAT **MINK** **SABLE**

Stepping out of the plane when we landed in Alaska felt like walking into a deep freeze. We were in the far northwest of North America, well inside the Arctic Circle where temperatures can fall to -40°C. We'd come to find some of the animals that can manage to survive in this inhospitable land, in particular the polar bear – top predator of the frozen north. This is what happened when the Deadly team braved the crippling cold of Alaska.

We settled into our accommodation in a little frontier town of 293 people and the next day drove off into the frozen wasteland in search of polar bears.

Arriving in the land of the polar bear. Brrrr - it's cold!!

When it's this cold the equipment suffers too, so even the camera has to wear a warm jacket.

It's -20°C and we're all wrapped up in layers of warm clothes. Look at the boots Rosie our director has on – they've got the thickest padding and she's wearing three pair of socks.

The local people catch a number of whales every year and use every scrap of the meat and hide that they can. The bones are then left in this wilderness where they attract animals. We're hoping a polar bear might come to take a look.

While we waited we were lucky enough to see lots of Arctic foxes. These little predators have needle-sharp teeth and, although they can catch prey, they're always up for an easy meal. They often follow polar bears to take scraps from their kills so seeing the foxes is a good sign.

Next day we were up early and headed off again to see what might visit the whale bones. This time we were rewarded with a sighting of a very rare animal indeed – the wolverine.

The wolverine is a member of the weasel family and one of the most ferocious creatures for its size. It's an elusive animal and rarely spotted so seeing it was one of our most amazing wildlife moments ever.

Snuggled up in our cosy coats we settled down to wait in the cars, cameras at the ready.

We had infra-red cameras too in case the bears came at night. With these we could film in total darkness. And we waited and we waited, but no bears came. Despite the cold some of us fell asleep. Sometimes things just don't work out so we went back to our base.

After four long days we were rewarded with our first glimpse of a polar bear and we forgot about the hard work and the cold.

Polar bears have an amazing sense of smell. They can sniff out prey under the ice and then punch through the ice to drag out the victim.

A skidoo - the best way of travelling across the ice. And we're following polar bear tracks!

What a magnificent creature and how incredibly lucky we were to see it.

Polar bear tracks.

SEA CREATURES WORDSEARCH

There's a whole world of
incredible creatures in the ocean.
Can you find the names of some of the animals the Deadly
60 team have seen while exploring the mysteries of the sea?

R	H	S	C	A	L	L	O	P	R	M	H
A	E	S	I	E	O	D	I	U	Q	S	W
L	U	B	I	T	N	Y	E	E	I	H	S
O	U	T	M	F	N	T	S	F	R	U	R
B	I	T	S	U	E	M	Y	T	P	H	F
S	T	B	T	A	C	L	U	O	E	T	S
T	A	T	O	A	L	U	T	S	S	R	T
E	N	T	D	E	E	C	C	T	S	I	D
R	P	I	J	U	O	E	X	A	U	E	N
S	E	A	U	R	C	H	I	N	E	C	L
H	S	I	F	R	A	T	S	R	I	S	R
E	L	C	A	N	R	A	B	F	N	T	S

OCTOPUS   MUSSEL   SEA CUCUMBER   OYSTER
STARFISH   SQUID   CUTTLEFISH   BARNACLE
LOBSTER   JELLYFISH   SCALLOP   SEA URCHIN

ANIMALS IN DANGER

We've encountered some extraordinary creatures on our Deadly 60 travels, but there is one species on our planet that is deadlier than them all – us.

A human with a few tools or weapons can kill more or less any other animal and we are also destroying natural habitats. Here are a few of our Deadly 60 animals that are in real danger.

TIGERS

These magnificent beasts once ranged across large areas of Asia, but now there may be as few as 2,500 left in the wild. People used to hunt tigers for sport and for their fur, but this is now against the law. The greatest danger is the demand for tiger body parts used in traditional Asian medicine. Poachers can get high prices for bones, teeth and other parts so while killing tigers is strictly against the law, it still goes on.

The WWF (World Wildlife Fund) is working with other organisations to secure more areas where tigers can live in safety in the wild and breed to increase the population. The WWF is also working for stronger anti-poaching measures and to enforce the ban on tiger products more strictly.

SHARKS

You might find it hard to believe but humans are a far greater danger to sharks than they are to us. Tens of thousands of sharks are killed every year. One of the biggest problems is the demand for shark fin soup, which is a great delicacy in some parts of Asia. The sharks are caught, their fins cut off for the soup, then their bodies are thrown back into the sea. Many sharks also die in nets set out to catch other species of fish.

A number of shark species are now struggling for survival and even the great white is considered to be vulnerable – which means it could become extinct if things continue as they are.

Conservation organisations are working to discourage people from buying and eating shark fin soup, and to develop safer fishing methods.

RHINOCEROS

All 5 species of rhinoceros are rare. Three, the Javan rhinoceros, the Sumatran rhinoceros and the black rhino, are in serious danger of becoming extinct. One subspecies of the white rhino is critically endangered but numbers of the other, the southern white rhino, have actually increased to more than 20,000, having previously fallen to about 50 animals in the wild.

Destruction of their habitat is one problem for the rhinos, but more serious is poaching for their horns. The horn is used to make luxury items such as dagger handles, but more importantly, ground horn is used in traditional Chinese medicine. It is believed to cure ailments such as arthritis, headaches and vomiting.

Organisations such as WWF and Save the Rhino are working to expand protected areas where rhinoceroses can live in safety in the wild, and to increase anti-poaching measures. They are also trying to reduce the demand for the rhino horns so there is no profit in poaching.

27

ANIMALS IN DANGER WORD SCRAMBLE

All of these amazing creatures are becoming increasingly rare and could disappear forever if their situations don't improve. Can you unscramble their names?

olalrig
(the largest ape)

_____

balehrteack uetlrt
(huge sea-living reptile)

_____

ngita apdna
(black and white bear)

_____

cbkal rhnorciseo
(large African mammal with a horn)

_____

lroap aerb
(white bear)

_____

lueb weahl
(largest sea-living mammal)

_____

egitr
(stripy big cat)

_____

ignat ailoldamr
(large armour-plated animal)

_____

atecehh
(fast-running cat)

_____

ansai ntaeplhe
(animal with a long trunk that lives in Asia)

_____

ogtanruna
(Asian ape)

_____

eret kagoraon
(tree-living marsupial)

_____

DEADLY TOP 10 FASTEST PREDATORS

Here is the Deadly team's list of the top 10 fastest predators – animals that rely on their incredible speed to catch prey. And speed doesn't just mean running – it can be a high-speed dive, a lightning strike with a claw or fang, or a super-fast tongue.

1 NORTHERN GANNET

This magnificent seabird soars over the ocean searching for prey. When it spots something it makes a spectacular high-speed dive from 30 metres above the surface and plunges into the water to seize fish such as mackerel.

- Enters the water at 100 kilometres an hour.
- Has a hard skull and special air sacs to protect its body as it hits the water.
- Strong dagger-like beak for seizing fish.

2. CHEETAH

The fastest land animal, the cheetah makes high-speed chases to catch prey such as fast-running gazelle. With its lean body and long legs, the cheetah is built for speed.

- Can accelerate from 0–100 kilometres an hour in under 3 seconds and reaches speeds of over 100 kilometres an hour – but can only keep going for a short distance.
- Has large lungs and nostrils so it can take in plenty of oxygen to fuel muscles.
- Supple spine, flexible hip and shoulder joints and huge leg muscles all help the cheetah run as efficiently as possible.

3. PEREGRINE FALCON

This bird of prey dive-bombs through the air to strike and catch other birds on the wing. It seizes prey in its sharp talons but kills with its hooked beak.

- Dives through the air at speeds of over 200 kilometres an hour.
- Such high speed could damage the lungs, but structures called baffles inside each nostril help to slow the intake of wind so the bird can breathe as it dives.
- Superb eyesight for spotting prey.

5

EYELASH VIPER

The colourful eyelash viper lives in Central and South America. It's small – only up to 76 centimetres long – but dangerous and it preys on small mammals and even hummingbirds.

- Has a pair of heat-sensitive organs on its head that help it detect warm-blooded prey at night.
- Lightning-fast reactions which enable it to strike its prey and inject its deadly venom before the victim has a chance to escape.
- Long sharp fangs.

4

TUNA

Torpedo-like tuna are some of the fastest fish in the sea. They are also some of the largest bony fish – the bluefin tuna is up to 2 metres long and weighs about 250 kilograms on average.

- Can swim at speeds of up to 70 kilometres an hour.
- Beautifully streamlined, tapering body cuts through the water with ease.
- Unlike other fish, tuna have a body temperature that is higher than the surrounding water, which increases their stamina and performance.

6 CHAMELEON

These reptiles may have the fastest tongues in the animal world. A chameleon hunts by using amazing camouflage and sitting motionless on a branch, watching for likely victims, then shooting out its tongue to capture any prey that comes close enough.

- Large eyes that can move independently for the best possible all-round vision.
- Feet that are perfectly adapted for grasping hold of branches, with 2 claws on one side and 3 on the other.
- Very long sticky-tipped tongue that can be shot forward by a system of muscles and bone in a fraction of a second.

7 DRAGONFLY NYMPH

Adult dragonflies are fast-flying predators and their young are speedy hunters too – but in water. The young, called nymphs, live in water for the first stage of their lives and catch prey such as tadpoles and even fish.

- Moves fast by a sort of jet propulsion, expelling water through its anus to shoot itself forward.
- Has a specialised lower lip, called a 'mask' which can be shot forward to grab prey in a fraction of a second.

9 STAR-NOSED MOLE

This little mole might not look like a fast mover, but it can hoover up small invertebrates with astonishing speed, thanks to its sensitive tentacles.

- Has 22 tentacles around its nose that sense electrical impulses given off by animals and help the mole find prey.
- On each tentacle are thousands of tiny receptive organs that help the mole build up a 3D 'picture' of its surroundings.

10 BLACK MAMBA

Probably the most dangerous snake in Africa, the black mamba moves fast to escape its own predators.

- Has been timed moving at 16–20 kilometres an hour.
- Can strike several times and inject large amounts of very powerful venom with each strike.
- The snake gets its name not from its skin but from the colouration of the inside of its mouth.

8 MANTIS SHRIMP

These crustaceans, also called stomatopods, are sharp-shooting ocean predators. They live in burrows and only come out to hunt for prey. There are many species, ranging in size from 2–30 centimetres.

- Uses large forelimbs to smash or stab prey with the force of a bullet.
- Speed is so great that it can shatter crab and snail shells.
- Incredible eyes that may be the most complex in the animal kingdom.

WHO'S THE MOST TOXIC?

This is a list of the Deadly team's top 10 most toxic animals. They all have deadly bites, stings, spit or spray and they are animals to keep well away from!

Can you guess what order they should go in and figure out the most toxic of all?

Here's a clue – number one is a tiny creature.

1 _____   **Giant centipede**

2 _____   **Sea krait snake**

3 _____   **Cone shell**

4 _____   **Poison dart frog**

5 _____   **Fat-tailed scorpion**

6 _____   **Skunk**

7 _____   **Komodo dragon**

8 _____   **King cobra**

9 _____   **Paralysis tick**

10 _____   **Sydney funnel web spider**

DEADLY ENCOUNTERS

We always take the best possible care when we're filming Deadly 60. We have to – we're dealing with some very dangerous creatures. But just occasionally things do get a bit scary. Here are some of our worrying moments.

STRONG BOA

Boa constrictors are snakes that live in tropical Central and South America and they can grow to a mighty 4 metres long. They kill by wrapping their strong coils around their prey and squeezing until the victim can't breathe and suffocates.

To test the strength of the boa, I put one round my neck. It wasn't too bad at first, but gradually the boa gripped me tighter and tighter until I was struggling for breath. And it wasn't that easy to remove the snake's powerful coils!

VAMPIRE BAT

This bat has incredibly sharp teeth that it uses to shave away a section of its victim's skin so it can lap blood from the wound. When I wanted to get a closer look at a vampire bat I was careful to put on thick gloves to protect myself. But the bat managed to turn its head round and bite me, right through the glove. Ouch!

ANGRY HIPPOPOTAMUS

The hippopotamus feeds on plants, not other animals, but it is aggressive, strong and responsible for more human deaths in Africa than any other mammal. I had ventured in my canoe into a river that was home to hippos, thinking that I could avoid them easily.

What I hadn't bargained for was that these massive animals could move so silently underwater. I didn't realise how close they were to me. I ended up with one hippo upstream and another downstream – I was trapped. In the end, I struggled to reach the riverbank as quickly as possible, where the team dragged me to safety. Phew! Narrow escape.

KILLER BEES

African honeybees are more dangerous than European honeybees because they are much, much more aggressive when defending their hives and will sting in greater numbers. Despite this, we wanted to take a closer look at a killer bee nest. I was kitted out in a protective suit, carefully taped up at the wrists and ankles so every inch of me was covered. I wore heavy rubber boots, gloves and a beekeeper's hat and veil. Dressed like this I climbed up to investigate a nest on a rock face. What a situation – thousands of killer bees in front of me and a 50 metre drop below me.

All went well for a while but the bees became increasingly disturbed by my presence. Then I made a mistake and knocked the nest – just slightly. The bees became seriously aggressive and started buzzing loudly. One stung me through my veil and then another and another. I'd seen enough – it was time to leave!

Can you fill in this criss-cross puzzle with the names of these insects?

TOP TIP – start with the longest words.

4 letters
WASP
FLEA
MOTH

6 letters
CICADA
WEEVIL

7 letters
FIREFLY

8 letters
LADYBIRD
MOSQUITO

9 letters
DRAGONFLY
COCKROACH
BUTTERFLY

11 letters
GRASSHOPPER

Q&A WITH STEVE AND THE TEAM

There's always lots everyone wants to know about the Deadly shows and how they're made. Here are some of the questions we're most often asked and our answers.

HAVE YOU TRAVELLED TO EVERY COUNTRY IN THE WORLD MAKING THE PROGRAMMES?

Not quite, but we have visited 101 countries so far, and Deadly has filmed on every continent except Antarctica. Hope we can go there sometime soon.

HOW MANY TIMES HAS STEVE BEEN INJURED?

Cross fingers, not that many. I've been stung a number of times and got some cuts and bruises but the only serious injury I've had was the time I was bitten by a spectacled caiman in South America. And that was only because I stepped on the animal by accident! I guess that shows that however deadly these creatures might be to each other they bear us no ill will and most are much more frightened of us than we are of them.

HOW LONG DOES IT TAKE TO FILM A DEADLY 60 EPISODE?

Depends on how lucky we are. Sometimes we can wait for days without catching a glimpse of the animal we're after; we've spent several weeks in the jungle trying to find a jaguar without even spotting a footprint. It's not as easy as you might think to find some of these magnificent creatures in the wild. On the other hand, some quite rare animals appear almost instantly – for example, giant river otters in Peru turned up on the lake before we'd even unpacked our equipment. That bit is just down to putting in the hours in searching and a bit of luck. It usually takes a week to film a show, then it has to be edited and finished off back in Bristol before it appears on your television screen.

WHAT'S YOUR FAVOURITE ANIMAL?

I find them all endlessly fascinating and there's always something new to learn about wildlife, but I guess one of my very favourites is the wolf. They're beautiful, intelligent animals and I like the way they work together as a group and communicate with each other. I'll never forget the first time I looked into a wolf's eyes – incredible.

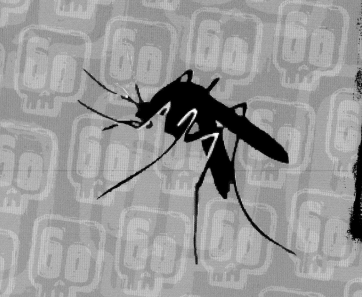

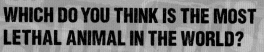

WHICH DO YOU THINK IS THE MOST LETHAL ANIMAL IN THE WORLD?

If we're talking about lethal to humans, it has to be the *Anopheles* mosquito. This tiny insect spreads deadly diseases and so kills many more people than a shark or a tiger ever could. The important thing to remember about most animals is that they would much rather stay well away from us than attack us. Predators are lethal for their prey but not usually to us – for instance, in 2002 just one person was killed by a shark – one. We want people to be interested in wildlife, not scared.

WHAT ADVICE DO YOU HAVE FOR YOUNG PEOPLE WHO WANT TO WORK WITH ANIMALS?

Start young by finding out as much as you can about animals – watch wildlife shows, read books, ask questions. And get out in your own backyard or local countryside as often as you can. Look for bugs, beetles, and spiders and find out about them. You'll find that their behaviour can be just as interesting as that of much larger animals. When you're old enough, ask if you can help out at your nearest wildlife centre. Always treat any animals you come across with respect and care.

WHAT ARE YOUR PLANS FOR THE FUTURE?

Well, Deadly 60 Series 3 has all been filmed, and it's the best yet! We have loads of wild record breakers, from the fastest fish in the sea, to the largest predator that's ever known to have lived, and from the world's most venomous snake, to the most venomous creature. It's going to be incredible! There's another massive project in the pipeline, but I'm not allowed to tell you what it is yet! I'm also writing lots and lots of books, including my first ever novel.

WHAT ANIMAL WOULD YOU MOST LIKE TO SEE?

The leopard seal in Antarctica – it's a formidable beast in one of the world's great wildernesses. Also the snow leopard. I've got crazy close to seeing one – at night in Bhutan I heard one snarl just metres away from me but didn't see it! Later this year I'm hoping to spend a few months in the mountains on the trail of the snow leopard.

ANY BIG EXPEDITIONS PLANNED?

I'd really like to climb another 8,000 metre mountain. Maybe K2 or Everest. And I'd like to make a big kayaking expedition as well, crossing an ocean or paddling the length of one of the world's biggest rivers.

43

PORTRAIT OF A PREDATOR: SCORPION

A scorpion is not an insect; it's an arachnid, which means it's related to spiders.

There may be nearly 2,000 different species, but only 30 or so of these are really deadly.

Scorpions have been around since before the days of the dinosaurs and were some of the first animals to live on land. Now they are found all over the world but are most common in warmer regions.

All are hunters and prey on other invertebrates such as insects and spiders. Some species of scorpion grow to 20 centimetres long and they will tackle lizards and mice.

When the scorpion hunts, it seizes its prey with its pincers, then may also swing the sting over it body and plunge it into its victim. The venom paralyses the prey so the scorpion can eat its meal in peace.

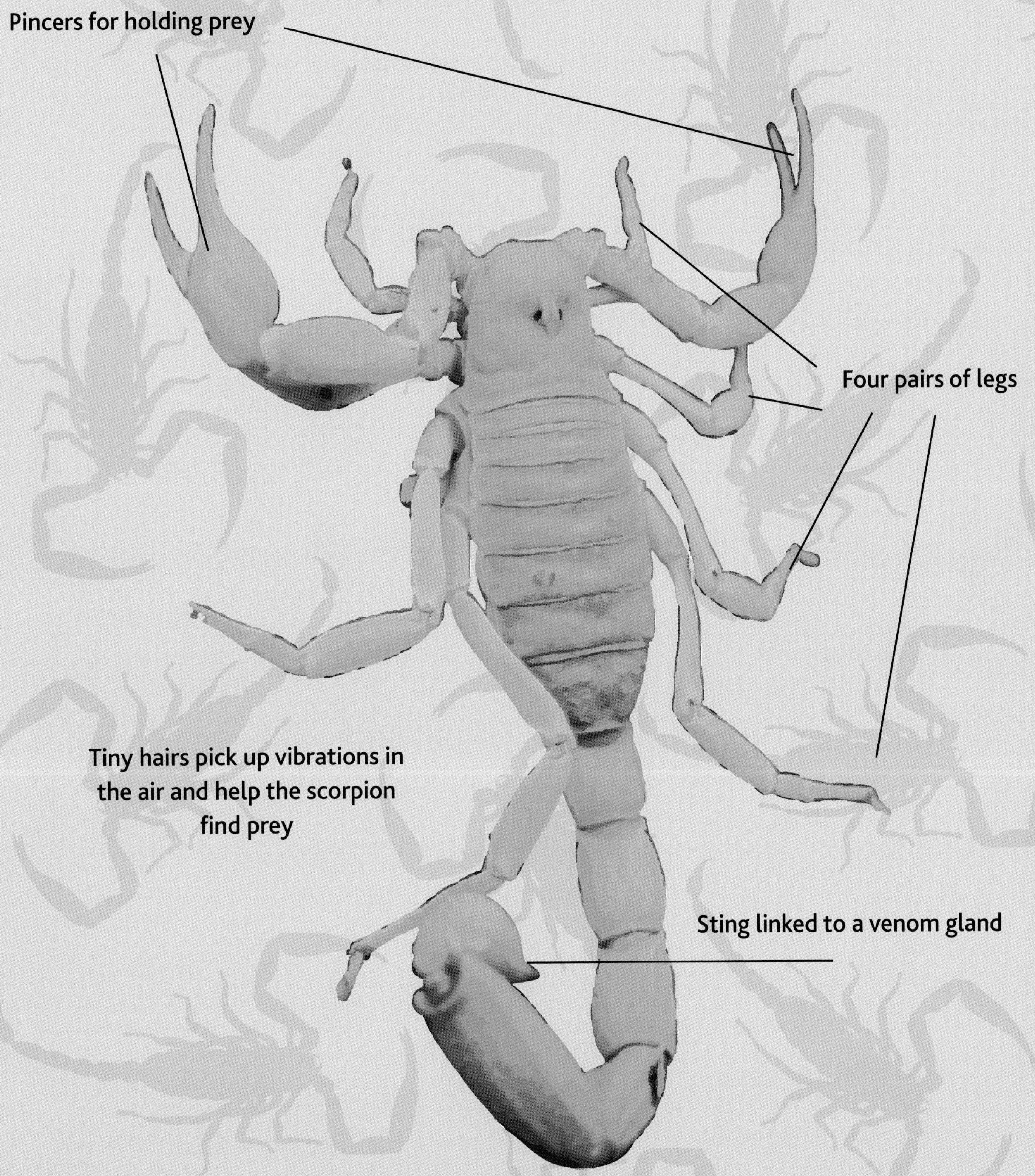

Pincers for holding prey

Four pairs of legs

Tiny hairs pick up vibrations in the air and help the scorpion find prey

Sting linked to a venom gland

Crocodile

Skill Level: Medium

The world's biggest reptile, the saltwater crocodile can grow to 7 metres or more. Its huge, powerful jaws contain 66 sharp teeth for seizing hold of its prey and tearing off chunks of flesh.

1. This doodle is made up of letters. Start by drawing a big letter 'C' for the head. Then add two more 'C' shapes for the body.

2. Then add two smaller 'C' shapes on each side, as shown, for the legs.

3. Draw a really big 'Z' for the mouth and a sideways 'Z' to make the lower jaw. Then add the curly tail.

4. Now add the ridges on the croc's back. Start at the tail and draw in two lines in each section, making them slightly wider apart as you get nearer the head. Draw an eye on the side of the crocodile's head.

5. Take your marker pen and go over your pencil lines to make them really bold. Add some 'V' shapes for the feet and claws and then draw some sharp teeth in the jaws.

6. Add some bold shading under the jaw and body, then make the eyes look mean by adding shading and some more lines underneath. Add in some lines to give the body a rough, scaly look.

DEADLY BATTLE: PREDATOR v PREY
GREY WOLF v ELK

Predators such as wolves might seem unbeatable, but prey animals have skills and tricks of their own to ensure that the hunters don't always succeed.

The Deadly 60 team filmed this epic battle between predator and prey in the rugged lands of Yellowstone Park in the United States. It was bitterly cold and there was thick snow on the ground, making it hard to move around – and all too easy to fall.

PREDATOR

The grey wolf has a lean, strong body and is built for speed and stamina. It is also highly intelligent and has bone-crunching teeth and superb senses.

PREY

The elk is also very strong and about 7 times the weight of the wolf. The male elk has massive antlers with sharp points that it can use to fend off an attacker.

Wolves hunt in packs, which gives them a better chance of bringing down large prey. But elk move in groups too, so there are lots of eyes and ears watching out for danger. Who do you think will win?

THE ACTION

The moment the elk get a whiff of danger and sense that a pack of wolves is near they start to run. Unfortunately for them, this is just what the wolves want, as it is easier for them to spot a weak member of the herd to target when the animals are on the move.

The wolves spot a female – she's smaller than the males and has no antlers. She is exhausted after the long chase and slightly lame. The pack catches up with her and pulls her down with their powerful jaws.

In their haste, the elk run down into a valley where the snow is deep and it's harder for them to move. The wolves manage to catch up and split an animal off from the herd. But it is a large male with huge antlers and the wolves move away and resume the hunt.

The hunt is over. Despite the elk's size and strength the wolves have won – this time.

Sharp canine teeth

Broad carnassial teeth for crunching bones

< WOLF SKULL

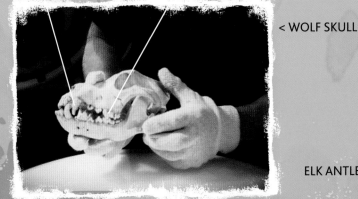

There can be as many as 7 of these sharp tines on an elk's antlers

ELK ANTLERS >

DEADLY 60 IN THE AMAZON

Amazon rainforest

South America

anywhere else on Earth. But catching them on camera is not as easy as it seems.

Before we went anywhere at all it took half a day to get the cameras and other equipment ready. Once all that was done we were ready for a walk in the forest, but this was not like the ones we know at home; the Amazon forest is inhabited by deadly snakes, huge tarantulas and all sorts of other creatures.

Filming Deadly 60 can be a challenge, not only because of the creatures we come across but also because of the places we travel to – one of the most extreme was the Amazon rainforest in South America.

After 2 days, 3 planes, 2 trucks and a ferry we found ourselves deep in the Amazon jungle, where there are more species of animal than

It's so hot and so humid it's like being in a steam room – day and night – and a nightmare for filming. When it rains, it really rains and it feels like it will never stop.

These conditions might be difficult for filming but it's heaven here for a naturalist like me and well worth putting up with the discomfort.

One of the creatures we really wanted to see was the pink river dolphin. And we'd decided to travel down river in a hydro-plane – a special plane that can take off on water. Very exciting indeed. We set off but as we flew over the vast forest, the clouds came down, torrential rain started and we had no choice but go back to base. No dolphins that day.

The next day we tried boat travel again and reached a place where we'd heard there were river dolphins. Sure enough there they were, and soon they were leaping round us, grabbing the fish we held up for them. This sequence takes up just a few minutes of television time but it took us 2 days in all to get – well worth it though.

Another sequence that took far longer than you'd think was the opening of the Amazon programme, which shows me diving off a riverboat. Easy, we thought. But the water wasn't deep enough, the boat was drifting and the sound wasn't right – it took us a whole morning to film the perfect dive, which is about 15 seconds of the programme. We finished in the nick of time – then it started to rain again!

DEADLY ART

Deadly 60 animals make fantastic subjects for all kinds of art projects, from masks to models and giant paintings. Here are some of the amazing projects we've come up with in Deadly Art. Have a look and be inspired.

Can you help this spider find her way to her prey?

DEADLY

PORTRAIT OF A PREDATOR: JAGUAR

The biggest cat in Central and South America, the jaguar is a sturdy, powerfully built animal with a large head and broad chest.

It generally lives in rainforest but can also be found in other habitats such as grassland.

This cat hunts by creeping stealthily towards prey and getting as close as possible before making a final lethal pounce.

It climbs well and is a surprisingly good swimmer too.

Prey includes large animals such as peccaries, tapirs and capybara but the jaguar will also eat smaller items such as fish.

Its jaws are so strong that it can kill by biting the skull of its victims and can even break turtle shells.

Excellent sense of smell, sight and hearing for tracking prey.

Powerful jaws and strong canine teeth for killing prey.

Rosette markings on its coat help the jaguar stay hidden in its jungle home.

Up to 1.8 metres long with a 75 centimetre tail and weighs 100 kilograms or more.

Stocky legs help it climb and swim well.

STAY AWAY FROM ME!

In Deadly 60 we've looked at lots of the ways animals attack their prey. But many creatures also have extraordinary ways of defending themselves – such as squirting blood from their eyes! Here are some of our favourites.

SQUIRTING BLOOD

Horned lizards live in North America and prey on insects such as ants. However, they themselves are a popular food item for many creatures including hawks, snakes, dogs and coyotes, so they need ways of defending themselves.

First, they try just staying very still in the hope that the attacker will go away. If that doesn't work, they can puff up their body like a spiny balloon. As a last resort, if the attacker persists, the lizard can spray blood from the corner of each eye. It's able to squirt the blood as far as a metre to warn off its enemy. The blood tastes really nasty and makes most predators go right off the idea of dinner.

CHEMICAL SPRAY

Bombardier beetles are only up to a centimetre long but have an amazing defence system. The beetle stores 2 kinds of chemicals in its body. If the beetle is in danger, these chemicals are released into a special area of the abdomen where they mix to create an explosive substance. This boiling hot mixture is sprayed out of the beetle's anus at the attacker and can burn and irritate.

HORNED LIZARD

STEVE WITH STINGRAYS

BARBED STING

The stingray is a huge fish with a flattened body that measures up to 2 metres across. A relative of the sharks, the stingray spends much of its time half-hidden in sand on the seabed. At the end of its slender tail is a sharp spine with serrated edges that's linked to a venom gland and this is used for defence, not hunting. If attacked, the stingray plunges its spiky barb into the enemy.

CONCEALED WEAPONS

The hairy frog lives in West Africa and has a very unusual way of defending itself. The bones of its back feet have additional claw-shaped sections that are normally covered with skin. If the frog is in serious danger, these bones break free and pierce through the skin so they can be used like claws to scratch and attack the enemy. Very cunning.

SMELLY SPIT

A large seabird, the fulmar feeds on fish and squid which it snatches from the water as it skims over the surface. The birds nest on cliffs and if any predator tries to approach the nest they will get a nasty shock. The fulmar spits out an oily substance at its enemy and it smells really, really terrible. In fact, the fulmar's name means foul gull.

MORE DEADLY ART

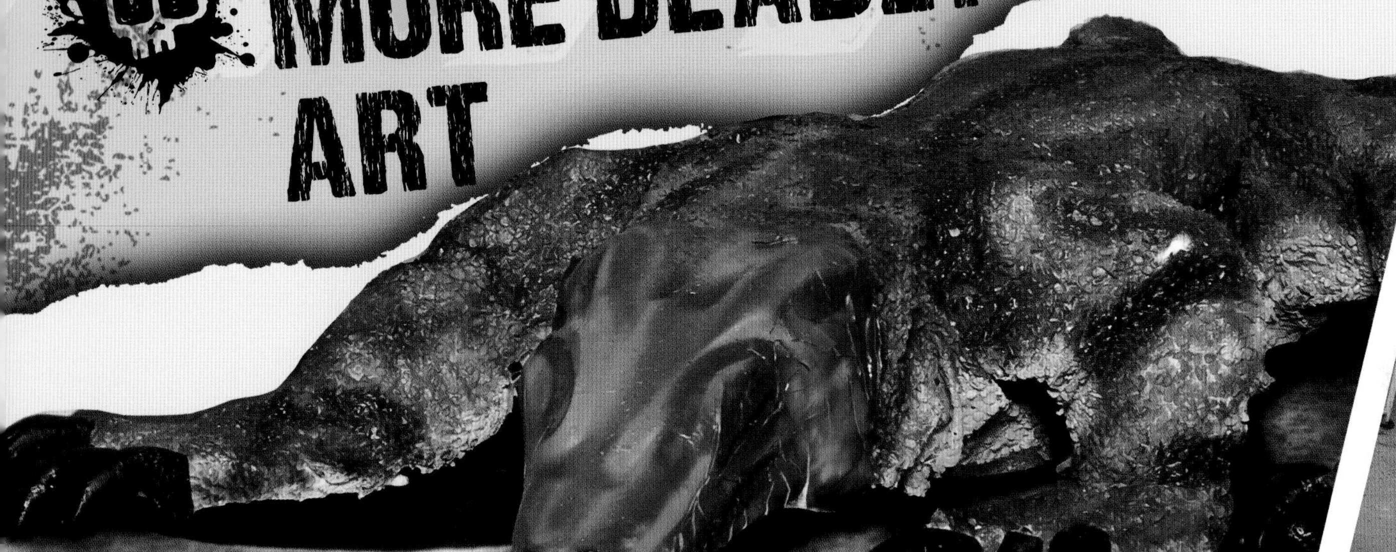

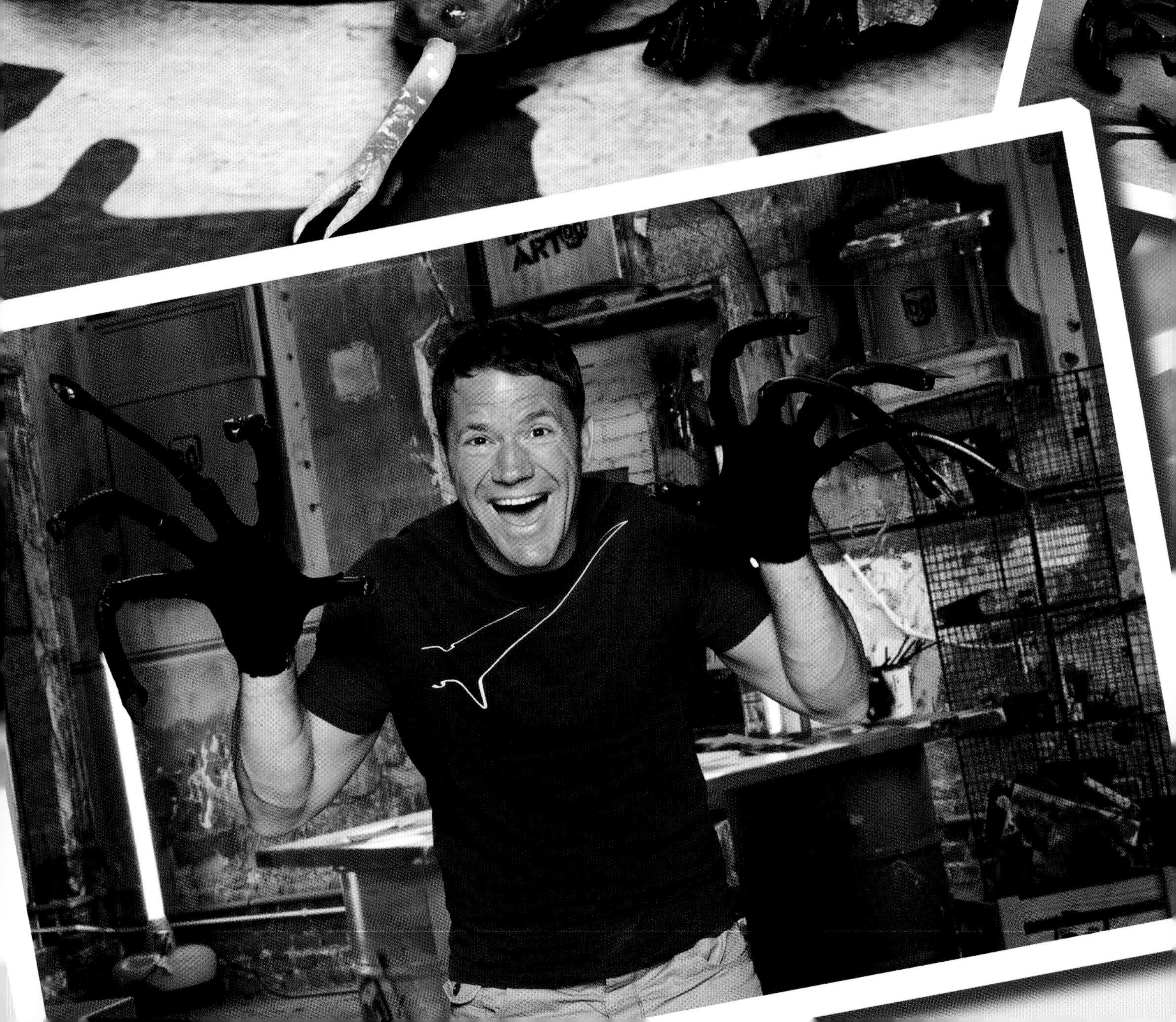

AFRICAN ANIMAL WORDSEARCH

DEADLY

Can you find the names of all these
African animals in this wordsearch?

E	L	G	A	E	D	E	N	W	O	R	C
S	G	K	M	C	V	A	G	C	J	H	F
N	H	A	G	H	T	T	A	R	G	D	V
F	C	B	O	I	S	F	N	O	O	R	F
E	I	M	H	M	E	A	E	C	R	A	L
N	R	A	T	P	E	A	Y	O	I	P	O
N	T	M	R	A	B	J	H	D	L	O	W
E	S	K	A	N	E	Y	N	I	L	E	D
C	O	C	W	Z	D	I	W	L	A	L	R
F	S	A	P	E	L	B	O	E	J	Q	A
O	O	L	A	E	I	H	R	S	X	L	A
X	C	B	B	M	W	Q	B	O	E	Y	Z

GORILLA	CHIMPANZEE	CROCODILE	WARTHOG
BLACK MAMBA	CROWNED EAGLE	BROWN HYENA	LEOPARD
AARDWOLF	WILDEBEEST	FENNEC FOX	OSTRICH

DEADLY BATTLE: PREDATOR v PREY
DAUBENTON'S BAT v YELLOW UNDERWING MOTH

Insect-eating bats, like other predators, have to find and catch food in order to survive. This deadly battle took place in a woodland in the UK at the dead of night and the Deadly 60 team were there watching.

The bat hunts at night but with echolocation it can build up a 3D picture of its surroundings through sound.

PREDATOR

Bats are the only true flying mammals and can twist and turn through the trees with the greatest of ease. Their wings are made of skin, supported by extra-long finger bones. The bat's special weapons are its sharp claws, needle-like teeth and a super-sense – echolocation.

PREY

The moth's stocky body is packed with flight muscles, making it strong, speedy and extremely agile in the air. It also has very acute hearing and can tune into the bat's clicking sounds with a simple ear on its body.

Its body is covered with tiny hairs that pick up the changes in air pressure made by the bat's flapping wings. All these clues could help the moth escape its hunter.

The echoes are channelled into the bat's ear and allow it to build a picture of the world around it and zone in on prey. The bat has picked up the moth's location and is heading towards it.

Meanwhile, the moth's special senses are tracking the bat's every move to help it evade capture. Just as the bat reaches the moth and strikes with its sharp-clawed feet, the agile moth drops through the air to the ground. It has escaped – this time! Another night it might not be so lucky.

THE ACTION

The bat is in flight, speeding through the night air, while emitting ultrasonic clicking sounds that we cannot hear. These bounce back off anything in their path – object or prey.

Piranha

Skill Level: Easy

This fish may be only 30 centimetres long, but it has razor-sharp, triangular-shaped teeth and can strip meat off bones with amazing speed. A creature to avoid!

1. Start by drawing a half-circle in the middle of your page. Add a triangle for the top fin, then two more for the side and tail fins.

2. Add a circle in the middle for one eye and a half-circle for the other eye.

3. Starting under the eye, add another triangle to make the fish's lower jaw.

4. Go over the fins with a black marker, adding zigzag lines and some detail inside for the spines. Make a nice thick black line around the eyes and add a small 'C' shape to each one for the pupils. Draw more zigzag lines on the top and bottom jaws for the sharp teeth. Lastly, add mean eyebrows over each eye.

COULD YOU JOIN THE DEADLY TEAM?

As you know from the programmes and from this book, life on Deadly 60 isn't all fun and games. We wait for hours in freezing cold, watching for creatures that may never appear, we wade into muddy rivers that are home to piranhas and we brave jungles full of stinging insects and deadly snakes. Are you adventurous enough to join our team?

Try this quiz and find out.

1 What would be your ideal holiday?
a Lying on the beach listening to your ipod.
b Visit to an adventure park.
c Backpacking through a wilderness, looking for exciting wildlife to photograph.

2 What is your favourite animal?
a Your pet cat.
b Horses.
c Grey wolf.

3 Do you think animals are:
a Cute and cuddly?
b Deadly and dangerous?
c Fascinating amazing creatures that should be studied and protected?

4 If you see a big spider in your garden, what do you do?
a Scream and run away.
b Admire it from a distance.
c Get as close as you can so you can get a really good look and take a photograph.

5 What's your favourite leisure activity?
a Playing computer games.
b Swimming and cycling.
c Walking and exploring in the country.

6 What do you think about wasps?
a A real nuisance when you're trying to have a picnic.
b You know they can sting so stay well clear.
c Interesting insects that do us a great service by catching lots of other insects to feed to their young.

7 Where in the world would you most like to visit?
a Hollywood.
b Grand Canyon.
c Amazon rainforest.

Score
Score 1 point for each (a), 2 points for each (b) and 3 points for each (c). See page 74 to find out what your score means.

QUIZ CROSSWORD

Work out the answers to this wildlife quiz and use them to fill in the crossword. Most of the answers are somewhere in this book.

1 Across What does a hippopotamus eat?
a Fish
b Fruit and nuts
c Grass

3 Across
See 12 across

4 Across Where does the sloth bear live?
a Asia
b Africa
c Australasia

8 Across & 7 Down Which creature squirts out a hot chemical spray to defend itself?
a Poison dart frog
b Praying mantis
c Bombardier beetle

9 Across How many legs does a spider have?
a Six
b Ten
c Eight

10 Across What kind of creature is a fulmar?
a Bird
b Fish
c Insect

11 Across Which animal does Steve think is the most deadly to humans?
a Tiger
b Tarantula
c Mosquito

12 Across and 3 Across Which of these seals is one of the most ferocious predators in Antarctica?
a Leopard seal
b Grey seal
c Harp seal

2 Down & 6 Down Which is the world's largest reptile?
a Saltwater crocodile
b Leatherback turtle
c Boa constrictor

4 Down What group of animals does a scorpion belong to?
a Arachnids
b Insects
c Amphibians

5 Down Which is the Deadly team's number one speedy predator?
a Cheetah
b Tuna
c Gannet

7 Down
See 8 across

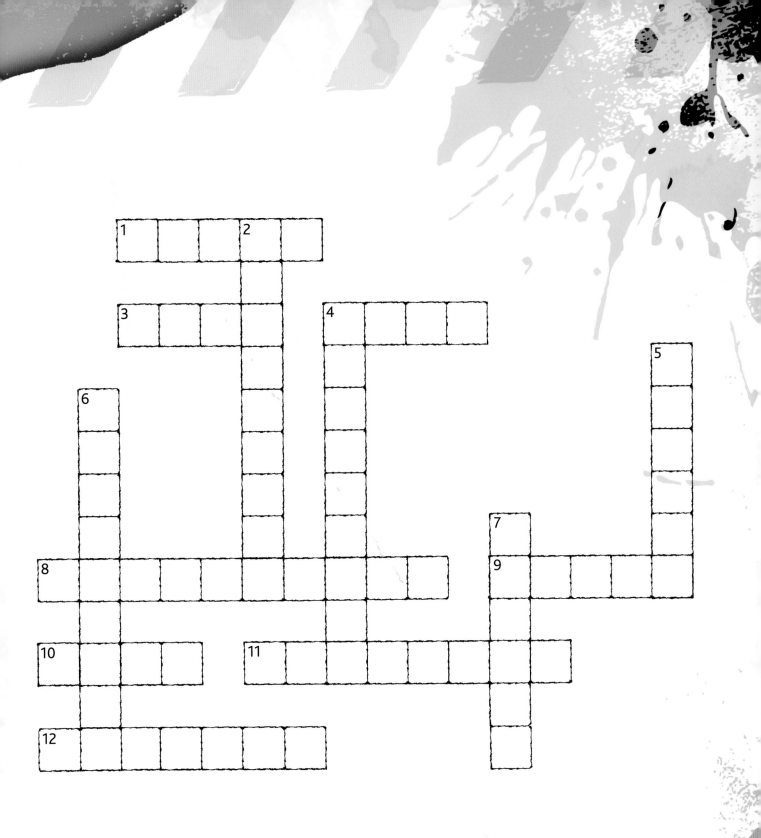

PUZZLE ANSWERS

p21 WEASEL WORDSEARCH

L	E	H	M	A	R	T	E	N	K	T	H
E	L	N	E	R	A	T	V	N	T	S	V
S	B	D	T	C	N	F	I	E	T	E	T
A	A	T	E	S	E	M	T	N	N	P	O
E	S	L	E	R	R	E	E	I	S	N	I
W	O	O	R	T	S	L	R	R	V	S	E
P	R	E	G	D	A	B	S	E	S	O	C
T	T	P	D	B	E	K	R	V	Q	B	Y
S	T	F	H	T	U	A	N	L	A	H	T
F	I	E	L	N	R	S	T	O	A	T	P
D	I	L	K	T	N	H	F	W	R	A	Y
H	R	E	T	T	O	A	E	S	E	Y	N

p25 SEA CREATURES WORDSEARCH

R	N	S	C	A	L	L	O	P	R	M	H
A	E	S	I	E	O	D	I	U	Q	S	W
L	U	B	I	T	N	Y	E	E	I	H	S
O	U	T	M	F	N	T	S	F	R	U	R
B	I	T	S	U	E	M	Y	T	P	H	F
S	T	B	T	A	C	L	U	O	E	T	S
T	A	T	O	A	L	U	T	S	S	R	T
E	N	T	D	E	E	C	C	T	S	I	D
R	P	I	J	U	O	E	X	A	U	E	N
S	E	A	U	R	C	H	I	N	E	C	L
H	S	I	F	R	A	T	S	R	I	S	R
E	L	C	A	N	R	A	B	F	N	T	S

p28–29 ANIMALS IN DANGER WORD SCRAMBLE

Gorilla (the largest ape)
Leatherback turtle (huge sea-living reptile)
Giant panda (black and white bear)
Black rhinoceros
  (large African mammal with a horn)
Polar bear (white bear)
Blue whale (largest sea-living mammal)

Tiger (stripy big cat)
Giant armadillo (large armour-plated animal)
Cheetah (fast running cat)
Asian elephant
  (animal with a long trunk that lives in Asia)
Orangutan (Asian ape)
Tree kangaroo (tree-living marsupial)

p35 WHO'S THE MOST TOXIC?

1 Poison dart frog

2 King cobra

3 Giant centipede

4 Paralysis tick

5 Komodo dragon

6 Cone shell

7 Skunk

8 Sea krait snake

9 Sydney funnel web spider

10 Fat-tailed scorpion

p53 SPIDER MAZE

p38 INSECT CRISS-CROSS

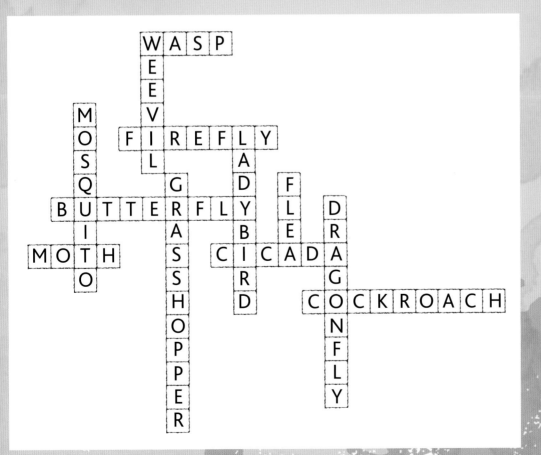

p63 AFRICAN ANIMAL WORDSEARCH

E	L	G	A	E	D	E	N	W	O	R	C
S	G	K	M	C	V	A	G	C	J	H	F
N	H	A	G	H	T	T	A	R	G	D	V
F	C	B	O	I	S	F	N	O	O	R	F
E	I	M	H	M	E	A	E	C	R	A	L
N	R	A	T	P	E	A	Y	O	I	P	O
N	T	M	R	A	B	J	H	D	L	O	W
E	S	K	A	N	E	Y	N	I	L	E	D
C	O	C	W	Z	D	I	W	L	A	L	R
F	S	A	P	E	L	B	O	E	J	Q	A
O	O	L	A	E	I	H	R	S	X	L	A
X	C	B	B	M	W	Q	B	O	E	Y	Z

p68 COULD YOU JOIN THE DEADLY TEAM?

7–9 Probably best to keep watching the programmes at home rather than joining the team.

10–14 You're interested in wildlife so keep it up. Watch lots of Deadly 60 programmes and read Deadly 60 books to find out more.

15–21 You're obviously passionate about adventure and wildlife so definitely on the right track. Keep finding out as much about wildlife as you can.

p70–71 QUIZ CROSSWORD

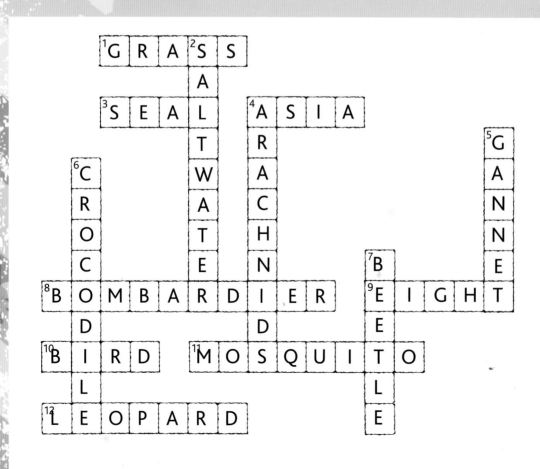

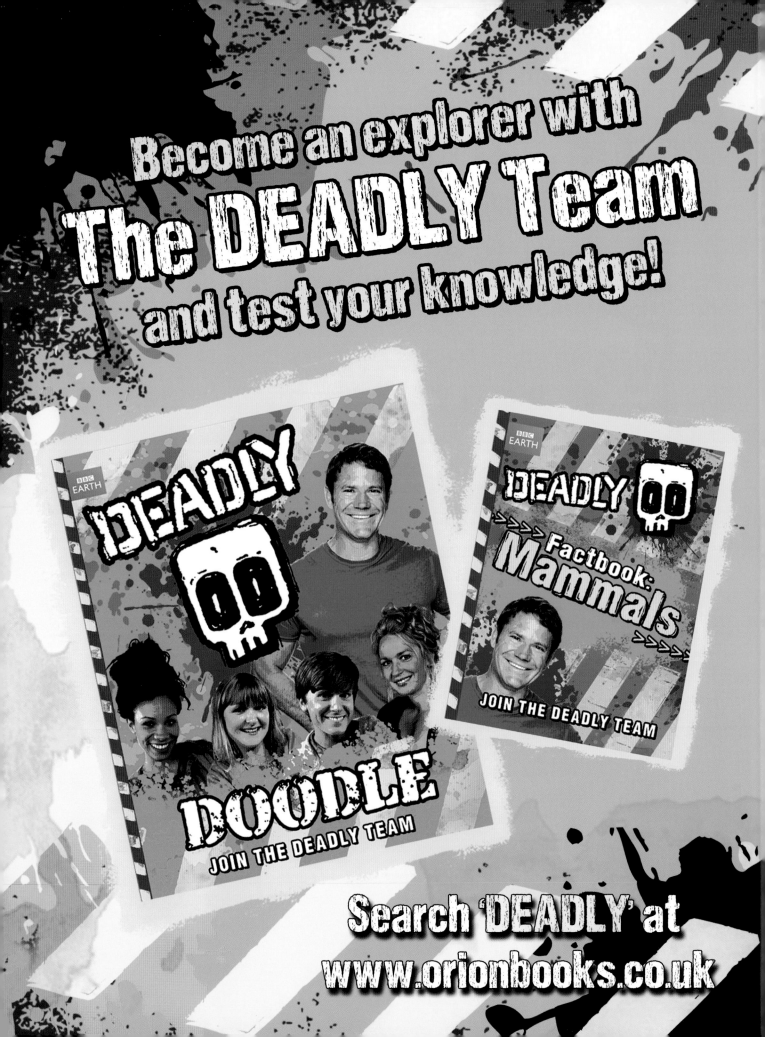

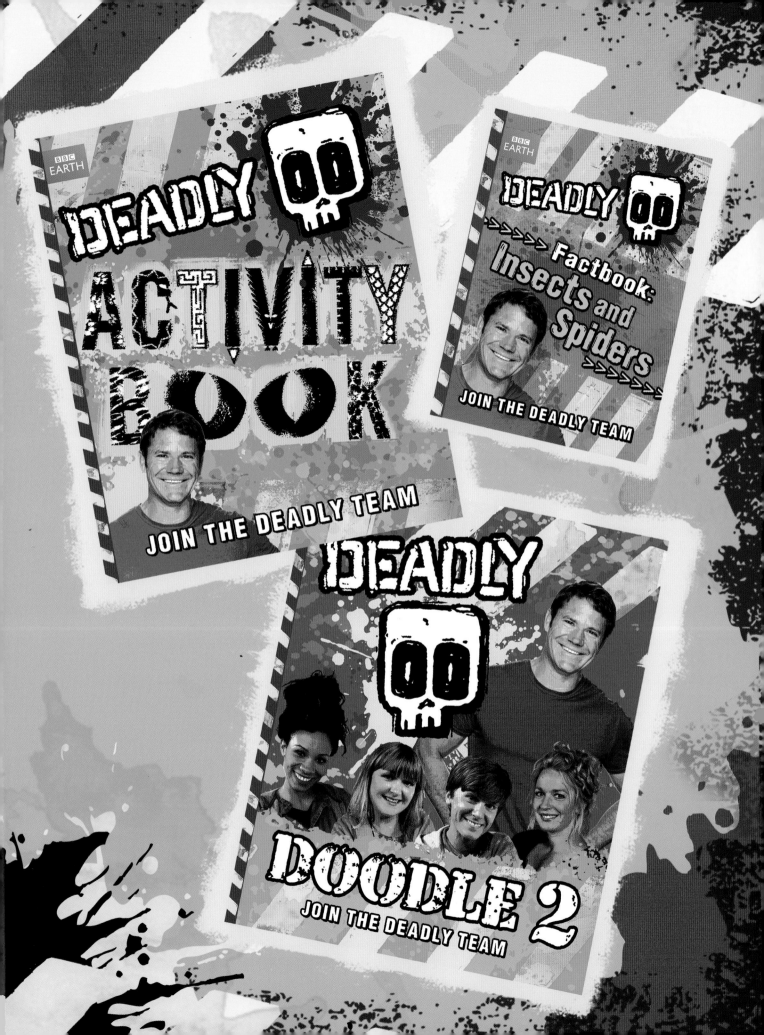